THE CHOCOLATE TEAPOT

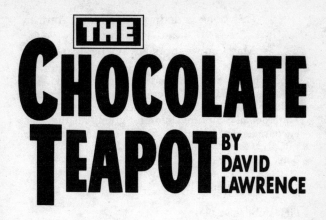

THE CHOCOLATE TEAPOT
BY DAVID LAWRENCE

SURVIVING AT SCHOOL

Scripture Union
130 City Road, London EC1V 2NJ.

This book is dedicated to Mark, Andrew
and Timothy.
May your teapots always be heat-proof.

Special thanks to: Chris and Maggie who provided a
'safe house' in Cardiff where most of this was written,
William Moore for the brilliant cartoons, and Becky
Totterdell at Scripture Union for giving me the
encouragement to start moulding *The Chocolate Teapot*

Book and cover design by Julian Smith

First published 1991
Reprinted 1991, 1992 (five times), 1993 (twice), 1994

British Library CIP Data
Lawrence, David
  The chocolate teapot
  1. Christianity. Religious life
  I. Title
  248.82

ISBN 0 86201 712 2

Printed and bound in Great Britain by
Cox & Wyman Ltd, Reading, Berkshire

All bible quotations, except where otherwise stated,
are from The Good News Bible – Old Testament:
Copyright © American Bible Society 1976; New
Testament © American Bible Society 1966, 1971, 1976.

Taking the lid off the chocolate teapot

There are lots of things that you can call a book. Here are some good names for books:

Hamlet
The Famous Five Go Roller Skating on Everest
My Little Donkey Annual 1997
Eric

Although these are all really good titles for books, this book is not called any of them. This book is called . . .

THE CHOCOLATE TEAPOT!!

Now of course it is obvious to you WHY this book is called *The Chocolate Teapot*. It isn't? Oh well, if you can't work it out for yourself I suppose I'd better tell you.

A teapot made of chocolate might look wonderful. It could be made to have a really ornate lid, interesting shape and long curving spout. You could even stuff it full of tea bags and all would be well, but the moment that the hot water is poured in disaster strikes and the chocolate teapot just melts away.

Sadly, this is a sort of picture of many young Christians. They look brilliant at church, at the youth group – even sometimes at home! But when the going gets tough and the heat is on at school, they just melt away and merge with the crowd.

This book is for chocolate teapots everywhere; people who perhaps feel failures because they've never really managed to stand up at school for what they believe, or for people who would like to know a bit more about living for Jesus at school.

Contents

Health warning This book may make you laugh. If it doesn't you're probably dead, or at least sickening for something quite serious.

Read this! You do not have to read the chapters in any particular order. Start with the ones that are about the subjects which most interest you at the moment.

With friends like those . . .

'Jaz', 'Daz' and 'Maz'. The three names brought a lump to my throat, a tear to my eye and the sort of feeling to my stomach that I'd once had after eating a double cheese burger and chips on a particularly rough sea crossing.

'Jaz' (really James), 'Daz' (really David) and 'Maz' (Matthew) were the self-appointed hard men of 3b. Their chosen purpose in life was to protect the whole class from outbreaks of Nurdish Behaviour, Naff Clothing and Wally Words.

If, for example, you were foolish enough to wear regulation school uniform, you were guilty of breaking the Naff Clothing rule and immediately became the target for comments like, 'Mummy dress you this morning, did she?'; if you did not watch Top of the Pops (or at least pretend that you did) you were obviously demonstrating Nurdish Behaviour and were immediately expelled from the 'in crowd'. As for 'Wally Words', the rules were simple:

1. Never pronounce the H at the beginning of words.
2. Never pronounce D or T at the end of words.
3. Occasionally miss D's or T's from the middle of words.
4. Wherever possible slur two or more words together.
5. Learn to use words that are meaningless to adults.
6. Never say 'please', 'thank you' or 'sorry'.
7. Swear as often as you can.

By the straightforward application of these rules you could say things like,

'Arsalrye, byate istree.'
(Translated: 'Art is all right, but I hate history.')

or

'See the foodie laznye? Brill wunni.'
('Did you see the football last night? It was brilliant, wasn't it?')

Anyway, the reason for my special fear of facing the terrible trio this morning was founded on three facts. Firstly my fluorescent socks were in the wash and I'd lost my trainers. I was therefore forced to resort to standard regulation school footwear – grey socks and Clarke's Commando shoes. Naff Clothing – guilty!

Secondly, I'd been to a church youth group meeting last night and not watched one minute of TV. Nurdish Behaviour – guilty!

Thirdly, after our maths lesson yesterday I'd made the mistake of being overheard saying, 'I'm terribly sorry for not completing my homework, Sir,' to Mr Kent, the maths teacher. Of course I should have said, 'Cawuz sikoni wunnee?' ('The cat was sick on it wasn't he?') which would have been a lie but far less 'Wally' – and possibly less Nurdish as well! Wally Words – guilty!

'Jaz', 'Daz' and 'Maz' . . . the self-appointed hard men of 3b.

So there I was, totally guilty and with no way out. Or was there? Maybe there was. I quickly ripped off my school tie and stuffed it in my bag. With my top shirt-button undone, my shoe laces trailing and my shirt hanging outside of my trousers I might just look scruffy enough to have a bit of 'cred' in the all searching eyes of 'Jaz', 'Maz' and 'Daz'. Mum wouldn't approve of course, but she won't know and I can always smarten myself up a bit before facing Mr Barnes, my class tutor. Phew, Naff Clothing crisis solved!

Nurdish Behaviour was easier; after all no one knew that I'd been to a church youth group last night. If I told a few well-placed lies (I call them half-truths to make myself feel better) no one need be any the wiser. OK, I was at home drinking Coke and watching the James Bond film just like everybody else.

But what to do about the allegations of Wally Words? After all there were eye-witnesses (or rather, ear-witnesses) to my apologies to Mr Kent. A possible way out of my dilemma was to deny that I'd meant it and to laugh at Mr Kent for being so easily taken in by my 'sincere' apology. Yes, in fact, if I'm rude enough about Mr Kent and if I throw in a few swear words, 'Jaz', 'Daz' and 'Maz' may well be sufficiently impressed to forget about the original offence completely!

Bible bit

It can be hard to do what is right at school when your friends (never mind your enemies) expect you to do something else. The pressure to do what they expect and to fit in with their way of doing things is enormous.

To try to do something which is different from what others are doing CAN make you the object of unkind comments or ridicule. It's sometimes far easier to blend in with what's going on, giving up what you know to be right in order to be accepted by the 'in crowd'. Right?

The trouble is that after you've sworn, lied, deceived your parents, told the dirty joke – or whatever – you feel guilty and ashamed. You know you've let God down and you're not sure what to do to put it right.

Well firstly, if you have failed, don't give up! You may have lost that particular battle to do what is right but you have not lost the entire war – that goes on for the rest of your life!

Have you ever read the bit in the Bible where Peter, one of Jesus' best friends, is watching Jesus after he has been arrested? In the courtyard where Peter is sitting there's a whole lot of people and some of them recognise that Peter is a friend of Jesus. Now, Jesus was becoming pretty unpopular at that time and Peter knew that if he was identified as a friend of Jesus, he'd become pretty unpopular too. So he had to think – fast. His solution was simple; lie and swear.

Peter was sitting outside in the courtyard when one of the High Priest's servant girls came to him and said, 'You, too, were with Jesus of Galilee.' But he denied it in front of them all. 'I don't know what you are talking about,' he answered . . . Another servant girl saw him and said to the men there, 'He was with Jesus of Nazareth.' Again Peter denied it and answered, 'I swear that I don't know that man!'

Peter recovered from that failure: although he let Jesus

down, Jesus gave him a starring role in the early church. So a few mistakes don't mean it's all over!

Practical pointers and handy hints

1 Of course it's not always true that your friends will only be doing bad things – for much of the time many of your friends will be fun to be with and fit in with. But because you are trying to live your life to please Jesus and your non-Christian friends are not, there will sometimes be a need for you to stop fitting in with them and be prepared to be different.

You see, you do not have to allow other people to run your life. You do not HAVE TO wear the sort of clothes that they wear, listen to the music that they listen to, go to the places that they go, watch the things that they watch, say the things that they say etc!! As a Christian you have chosen Jesus to be the Lord of your life. That means that he is the boss – and that makes a lot of sense, because he invented life, so he knows what advice to give you to make YOUR life as good as possible. The 'Jaz's', 'Daz's' and 'Maz's' of this world may have their own ideas on life, but they are not God, so it doesn't make much sense following them and their way of doing things if it contradicts what God says.

Sometimes life gives you a basic choice; please your friends or please God. The decision is yours.

2 Make sure that you have some friendships with other Christians in your school. Then if the going gets a bit tough with your non-Christian friends you will not be all alone. You can turn to your Christian friends for support and encouragement. You could even pray together about the situation!

3 Be ready to be positive! If your friends are doing something which you feel uneasy about, why not suggest a positive alternative? For example, maybe there's nothing much to do at lunch-time and you and your friends often get bored. To liven things up a bit they start picking on some younger pupils, which you know isn't right but sometimes join in with anyway. Perhaps if you and your friends had something constructive and interesting to do at lunch-times you would not find it so necessary to entertain yourselves at the expense of other people!

So why don't YOU try suggesting a more creative way of spending the lunch hour. Suggest joining a lunch-time activity (most schools have some – if yours doesn't how about starting one?!) or take in a board game to involve your friends.

4 Get your faith in God out into the open. It is always a mistake to hide what you believe, hoping that sometime in the future you will find it easier to tell your friends that you go to church, believe in God, pray and read the Bible. It doesn't get easier, it gets harder the longer that you leave it.

5 Maybe some of your 'friends' will laugh at you because you go to church. That's only because they do not understand who God really is and what following him is really all about.

The thing is that if they are really FRIENDS then they will not laugh at you but will accept the fact that you believe something different to them. Friends who do not allow you to be yourself with them, but want you to be someone that you are not, are really not very good friends at all; you're probably better off without them!

Think about it

1 In the space below, write down the names of your three best friends at school. Write next to each name what it is that you like about that person.

2 Still thinking of your three best friends, is there anything about your friendship with them that causes you to feel uncomfortable? (For example, do they expect you to join in with things that you know upset God? Do they use language which is offensive? etc.) Pray that God will give you the strength to stand up for what you know to be right and to be a good influence on your friends.

3 In the space below write down one thing that you want to do differently in your friendships at school as a result of reading this chapter.

A testing time

Some poor misguided individual once said that 'school days are the happiest days of your life.' Well it's true enough that some school days are happy (for example, the school day before half-term holidays, the school day before Christmas holidays, the school day the boiler blew up and we all got sent home early etc, etc!!). But whoever it was that made that claim obviously did not have a school day on which he was expected to use MY brain to do one of Mr Kent's maths tests! Pitting my brain against Mr Kent's maths test did not make me happy. Fed-up; yes. Depressed; yes. Happy; no.

Maths tests are OK provided that:

(a) you can make yourself see the point in doing them,

(b) you can get your brain cells around the answer,

(c) you've done at least some work in the last two weeks' maths lessons.

To be honest, I had problems on all three counts. With regard to point (c), I had been a teensy bit lazy in the last few maths lessons, not having worked on the set tasks with much enthusiasm at all. This was partly due to the fact that I didn't really understand what I was supposed to be doing and partly because I had a very intricate felt-pen and biro decoration to complete on my pencil case (which obviously took priority over maths work).

As for point (b), I couldn't even get my brain cells around the questions never mind the answers. I always try to read the question calmly at first, because I hope that if I read them slowly enough the words will, in some miraculous way, make sense to me. But then with an ever deepening sinking feeling inside I realise that I am bound for failure once again. Achieving a maths mark in double figures (all tests are marked out of 50) was about as likely as Iceland winning the Eurovision song contest or Michael Jackson growing up to be normal (or growing up at all come to that!).

And so to point (a). Some maths work will, I am sure, be very helpful in later life; I just wish we could get to that bit soon! So many of the problems that we have to solve just have nothing at all to do with real life. Take, for example, the following:

PROBLEM

Your mother goes to Tesco's with £50.00 in her purse. She buys groceries that cost £27.87 and leaves the store. On her way home she remembers that she forgot to buy any pet food so she returns to the shop to buy some. She purchases three tins of dog food at 46p each and a box of Miaow Krunchies at 96p. You normally receive £2.00 a week pocket money. When your Mum finally returns from shopping, how many weeks' pocket money does she have in her purse?

Now I have difficulties with this type of problem, because:

(a) my Dad does the shopping on his way home from work on a Friday, so my Mum never goes to the supermarket,

(b) Mum never has more than £10.00 in her purse because she always pays for everything by cheque,

(c) there is no Tesco supermarket in our town,

(d) our weekly shopping bill is more like £60.00 than £27.87,

(e) we do not have a dog and our cat died last week,

(f) and as for £2.00 pocket money a week!!

I'm sure that you can see the reasons for the brain-strain caused by trying to get to grips with this sort of puzzle. Here is another example from our recent maths test:

PROBLEM

Each time you fill the bath, the water flows in at the rate of 15 litres per minute through the cold tap and 12 litres per minute through the hot tap (when they are fully turned on). The water flows out through the plug hole at the rate of 8 litres per minute and the bath holds 500 litres before it overflows. It you were filling the bath with both taps on and the plug out, how many minutes would it be before the bath overflowed?

. . . how many minutes before the bath overflowed?

Now doubtless to some people this is an everyday situation and so they have no problems in tackling it as a mathematical exercise. However I must, once again, admit that I have certain problems with applying my brain to this situation. My problems may be explained thus:

1. I always take a shower so have little experience of bath taps.
2. If I WERE to a take a bath I would not turn both taps fully on since this is bound to result in a freezing cold bath.
3. Even if I DID turn both taps fully on, I would not attempt to fill my bath with the plug out.
4. Even if I DID turn both taps fully on and DID leave the plug out I would not allow the bath to get anywhere near overflowing because my Mum would beat me around the head with the back-scrubber.

Although I may be seeming to make light of my brain's struggles, there is a serious side to it. You see, when your brain doesn't manage to do what teachers want it to, the world can begin to seem an unhappy place. So-called 'friends' start to make fun of you (Question: 'What's the difference between David's brain and a dustbin?' Answer: 'At least a dustbin's got rubbish in it'), teachers try to 'encourage' you ('You'll just have to stay in at break time to do it all again.') and parents begin to give up on you becoming the little genius that they always hoped you'd turn out to be!

To be honest I'm beginning to get fed up with being so useless and just wish that 'Failure' wasn't my middle name. Why couldn't I have been born to be successful and brainy?

Bible bit

Well, it all depends on what you mean by words like 'successful', 'useless' and 'failure'. You may have been conned into believing that successful human beings are the ones with loads of brains and loads of friends but the truth is different!

Some of the people who became the greatest successes in the Bible were the weediest failures in the eyes of other people at the time. Take Gideon, for example. He was hiding from his enemies when God sent an angel to talk to him. Gideon describes himself as a member of the weakest group in his tribe and as 'the least important member' of his family! In other words Gideon was the pits in his own eyes – a coward and an unimportant member of an unimpressive family! Poor Gideon.

But just listen to how God sees him. God says to this jelly-heap of a man, 'The Lord is with you, brave and mighty man.' Gideon probably wondered who God was speaking to!! You see the truth is that God does not see ANY human being as unimportant, worthless or useless – not even a Gideon or a you! No matter what other people may say, do or think, and no matter what you may even have begun to believe yourself, there are two strong reasons why God thinks you're an OK person.

Firstly, you can know that you are an OK person because you are the most fantastically designed, most wonderfully advanced and most incredibly complicated part of God's world! Your body – even if it can't do Mr Kent's maths tests or win the high jump – remains something that modern science cannot copy. No robots or computers anywhere in the world can imitate the complex functions of your human body. So when

God looks at you he doesn't see FAILURE stamped across your face, because you (and every other human being) are the best thing that he ever created. He looks at you with pride, pleasure and admiration simply because you are part of the human race – that's enough.

John wrote these words: 'God loved the world so much that he gave his only Son, so that everyone who believes in him may not die but have eternal life.' He did NOT write these words: 'God loved the brainy people and attractive people in the world so much that he gave his only Son, so that anyone with 8 GCSEs, 3 A-Levels and loads of friends may not die but have eternal life'!!

In fact Jesus made it his business to befriend people who everyone else called failures. He went out of his way to spend time with unpopular, even hated people – like Zacchaeus. Surely he's got loads of time for people who struggle at maths, sport, speelling etc?

The second reason why God does not give up on you as a hopeless case is because he can see the future. He knows that you are an extremely useful human being and there are things that need doing in the world that you are just the person to do.

Just like God saw that Gideon (El Wimpo) was the man to defeat the armies of the Midianites (read about it in Judges 6–8): he saw that the murderer Moses was just the man to free his people Israel from the grip of slavery in Egypt. Just as Jesus chose the unpredictable, speak-now-think-later Peter as a disciple, and called him 'a rock', God chose the nervous, young, inexperienced Jeremiah to preach strong sermons to Israel and the surrounding countries. God seems to get a real kick out of choosing people who think that they are useless, or who others think are useless, and using them for something important and useful.

Even Jim couldn't have fixed it for Gideon to be a military hero, or Moses a great leader, or Peter to be a rock-like dependable person, or Jeremiah a powerful preacher; but God could and did.

Now believe this – God'll Fixit For You. Whatever the state of your test results, God can make your life useful and successful IF you are willing to do what he asks you to.

Practical pointers and handy hints

1 Refuse to believe any opinion about yourself EXCEPT God's opinion – that as a human being you are valuable, successful and useful.

2 If you find certain aspects of school work difficult, don't just give up; ask your teachers why they think you find it hard, and how you can begin to cope a bit better.

3 Make your aim each day to do your best, NOT to get full marks or be top of the class. If your aim each day is to do your best then every day can be a success because you can always go home knowing that you HAVE done your best (whatever marks you got for it). If your aim is to be cleverest, fastest, neatest – or whatever – you will frequently be disappointed when others beat you.

4 Look out for the things that you CAN do at school, and develop those as much as possible. God has made everybody good at different things, so try to discover what it is that God has given you the ability to do, and try to do it as well as possible. Enjoy what you can do and don't get too worried about what you can't.

5 Do all that you can to encourage other people in your class who are struggling with certain subjects and activities. Never mock other people who find the work difficult (you know how much you hate being laughed at). Congratulate them for the things that they are good at.

Think about it

1 In the space below write the name of someone in your class who struggles with the work and who you could try to encourage.

2 Think about any areas of difficulty which you experience with your school work. Are you doing your best at it? If so you are succeeding!

Teachers!

The trouble with teachers is that they are always right – even when they're wrong! Take 'Boggers' for example. (Actually 'Boggers' is really called Mister Jones, but his hair stands up like the bristles on a bog er . . . toilet brush, hence his nickname.)

'Boggers' takes us for science and he is, by common agreement, a bit of a wimp – at least he is on some days. On other occasions he acts like a cross between Rambo, Hitler and Albert Einstein! But that's precisely the problem – you never know where you stand with him. One lesson he can be really soft and anyone could get away with murder (well, almost) and the next lesson he goes all strict on you and starts giving out lines and detentions like they were past their sell-by date.

Of course 'Boggers' isn't the only teacher with his own funny little ways; all teachers take a bit of getting used to. In fact that's another problem with teachers – they're all different. There's the 'line-up-outside-the-door-and-you-can't-come-in-until-you're-quiet' sort and there's the 'if-you-get-there-before-me-go-in-and-get-on-with-something' sort. There's the 'OK-let's-discuss-this-together' sort and the 'don't-answer-back-I'm-in-charge-here' sort. Then again there's the 'right-I-warned-you-off-to-the-Head's-study' sort and the 'I'll-pretend-I-didn't-hear-that' sort. Do you get the picture? Worst of all is when, for no good reason, a teacher goes all heavy-duty on you – like last week in music.

Mrs Glen is pretty well-liked, for a teacher. She always tries to make the lesson interesting and we all really like it when we work in groups with percussion instruments composing music. Last Thursday was supposed to be such a practical lesson, but when we got there Mrs Glen told us that we'd have to carry on with our writing topic. Apparently there was an exam in the hall next door to the music room and we had to be quiet. Well, we were really disappointed and a few of us said so.

As a protest some people never really made any attempt to get on with their writing project but just sat there and chatted to each other. After about ten minutes Mr Morris, the violin teacher that visits the school, came in and wanted a word with Mrs Glen. She went outside to talk to him, threatening all sorts of terrible punishments for anyone who misbehaved in her absence. The minute the door closed behind her, chaos broke out. The precise sequence of events went like this:

1. James falls off his chair (accidentally!) and knocks Sandra's desk.
2. Sandra (normally a quiet girl) thumps James becaue he has jogged her and spoilt her drawing of a tuba.
3. James pushes Sandra and she falls over onto the cake that Sharon has just baked in cookery.
4. Andy (Sharon's twin brother) and Keith (who fancies Sandra) jump on James (who fancies himself) to the accompaniment of loud cheering from everyone else.
5. The glockenspiel on Mrs Glen's desk gets knocked over, its tuned bars clattering to the ground like heavy-metal confetti.

. . . I emerge with a handful of dismembered glockenspiel bars.

6. I crawl under her desk to pick up all the bits.
7. Mrs Glen re-enters the room.
8. Everyone else sits down and resumes work as though nothing had happened.
9. I emerge from under her desk with a handful of dismembered glockenspiel bars.

Now, I ask you; what would you have thought? Well, it will surprise you to know that Mrs Glen thought I, me, myself, personally had been up to no good. What is more, she said so – in no uncertain terms. Which proves my point about teachers; even the best of them can go completely over the top, for no reason whatsoever. Well, I can't see a reason, can you?!

Bible bit

It may be hard to believe this, but every single teacher is a human being! They don't sleep in the staff room at nights, plugged in to the power supply like Rechargeable Humanoid Education Machines. They go home, eat, sleep and watch TV like everyone else. What is more they have feelings! They can be happy and cheerful but they can also get fed-up, frustrated, angry, disappointed and hurt inside – just like real people. What is more, God loves them just as much as he loves you, and he wants YOU to show them his love.

Hang on a minute; love teachers?! NO – don't shut the book, read on.

You see, God is concerned about every human being and he wants his followers to share that concern. In fact – and this is going to blow your socks off if you've never thought about it before – God works out how much we love him by the way we treat other people (including teachers). Get your brain cells around these Bible verses:

If you laugh at poor people [or teachers], you insult the God who made them (Proverbs 17:5).

If someone says he loves God, but hates his brother [or teacher], he is a liar. For he cannot love God, whom he has not seen, if he does not love his brother [or teacher], whom he has seen. The command that Christ has given us is this: whoever loves God must love his brother [teacher] also (1 John 4:20–21).

You see, every single human being is a bit like a photocopy of God. The Bible says that humans (you, me and teachers!) are made to be like God. It is true that all of us human beings manage to cover up our God-likeness by all sorts of unkind and bad behaviour. Maybe we are like a photocopy of God that got a bit crumpled and smudged as it came out of the machine so that his image in us has got a bit spoilt, but that does not alter the fact that every person has something of God about them. Therefore, when we laugh at other people, we laugh at the image of God in them; when we are rude to them we are rude to the image of God in them; when we refuse to help them we refuse to help the image of God in them. Of course the opposite is also true. When we help them God sees it as helping him; when we are kind to them, God counts it as a kindness done to him, and so on. Jesus made all this very plain in the story about the 'Sheep and the Goats'. (Read it for yourself in Matthew 25:31–46.)

So what has all this got to say to us about 'Boggers', Mrs Glen and all teachers (good and bad) every-where? Well, it means that whatever other people's attitude to teachers may be, Christians are expected to love them, because however successfully they manage to hide it, all teachers are human and there-fore designed by God to carry his likeness. To put it even more plainly (with apologies to John!) . . .

If someone says he loves God, but hates 'Boggers', he is a liar. For he cannot love God, whom he has not seen, if he does not love 'Boggers', whom he has seen. The command that Christ has given us is this: whoever loves God must love 'Boggers' also!!

Of course this is easy to say but difficult to do. How do you love teachers? Offer to do all their marking for them? Clean their Citroën 2CV at break? Well maybe not! Here, to get you started, are some. . .

Practical pointers and handy hints

1 Remember why you are going to try to love them. Not to gain extra marks in the test and certainly not to impress your friends! They will probably not see things in the same way as you do. That is inevitable because you are trying to do what God wants and they may not be. Be assured, though, that God sees what you are doing, understands why you are doing it and is really chuffed to bits when you try to do what he wants.

2 Try to see things from your teachers' point of view. For example, in the story above, Mrs Glen may have jumped to the wrong conclusion but if you were Mrs Glen how would YOU feel if you were tired, your lesson had been disrupted by exams in the hall next door, several people in the class were being awkward, you

get interrupted by an unhappy violin teacher moaning about his pupils not turning up on time and then you re-enter your classroom to find someone crawling under your desk with a handful of expensive musical instrument?! Let's be honest and admit that any one of us would have found our patience being stretched a bit thin!!

3 Try never to do or say anything to a teacher (or about a teacher) that you would not like done or said to you. Why should they put up with behaviour from you, that you yourself would find hurtful?

4 Teachers make mistakes (because they are human!). Don't bear grudges against them and don't keep on repeating their mistakes to others so that you can all have a really good laugh at their expense.

5 Have the courage to own up to your mistakes and to say sorry when you are responsible for any bad behaviour.

6 Pray for your teachers.

7 If you have enjoyed a particular lesson or activity it would encourage your teacher to get a 'thank you' occasionally. Try and give out one 'thank you' a day; it won't hurt too much, I promise!

Think about it
1 In this space write in your own words one thing that you have learnt about how to relate to teachers.

2 In this space write one thing that you intend to do to improve your relationships with teachers.

3 In this space write the name of one teacher who you find difficult to get on with and who you could begin to pray for.

Pick on someone your own size

The thing that I like best about Sports Day is the night before it.

On the night before Sports Day I am the school's champion athlete. I beat the school's fastest runner in the 100 metres sprint, breaking the finishing tape just before the other runners manage to leave their starting blocks; I smash the school long jump record by 15 metres (give or take a metre) and I hurl the discus so far that Miss Harrison, the teacher in charge of the event, has to get her battered Mini from the car park to retrieve the discus for the next competitor (who manages a measly 25cm). The teachers are forced to cancel the 800 metres when the other competitors all withdraw rather than be humiliated by being beaten by me and my Mum is moved to tears of joy and pride as I win the 4×100 metres relay race on my own. At the end of the afternoon's events the Head makes an emotional speech praising my athleticism, my versatility, my stamina and my humility as he kneels at my feet to present me with the 'School's Outstanding Sportsperson of the Decade' award. Later, at home, my Dad puts up another five shelves in my bedroom to display the trophies that have just been delivered by Securicor.

That, as I said, all happens (in my imagination, of course) on the night before Sports Day. On the actual day itself the reality is, well, sort of different.

To start with I must admit that I'm not actually very fit. I can't really understand that, since I exercise regularly (I walk to the sweet shop at least twice a day) and I eat loads of fitness foods (like Mars bars and Diet Coke for instance). Anyway, since I do not seem to be the owner of a super-fit body I thought it best this year to enter an event that required the minimum of movement.

Hurling my body through the air in the jumps didn't seem too appealing, nor did attempting to sprint, run or hurdle my way into the record books: but how about throwing something? Yes, surely the shot putt would be the ideal event for an athlete such as me. All you have to do is stand still, then in a sudden, short burst of activity you chuck this sort of cannon-ball-like object as far as you can. If you can also grunt loudly as you release the shot, this gives the impression to watching parents that you are putting huge amounts of effort into the event. This always goes down well and may even result in a congratulatory Mars bar whether you win (unlikely) or lose (strong possibility).

Having entered for the shot putt and having practised by throwing half bricks at our next-door neighbour's cat (which happily stayed out of range of the missiles whilst becoming increasingly terrified by my ever-improving grunts) I arrived at school feeling pretty confident. Life took a sudden and terrible turn for the worse, however, when I read the list of competitors that I was to throw against. There were just three names in the shot putt column; Darren White's, James Kirkby's and mine. Darren White posed no threat since he was about as athletic as me, but James Kirkby (better known as 'Jaz') was another matter.

'Jaz' was one of those people who got his own way. One of those people that you did not argue with (not twice anyway). 'Jaz' was not into polite conversation or reasonable discussion in any big way. He was more into hitting people, threatening people or preferably both. He was in some ways a sort of humanoid Winnie the Pooh (the bear with very little brain) without any of Pooh's more lovable characteristics – although no one in their right mind would tell him so! His shortcomings in the world of study and his equally dismal record of sporting achievements did nothing to diminish his desire to perfect his skills of aggression and nastiness. That being as it may, my immediate problem was how to compete against 'Jaz' in that afternoon's shot putt competition. If I pulled out he would probably do me over for being a chicken, but if I competed and beat him (unlikely but not impossible) . . . well, I might as well have booked my hospital bed then and there. The only way to keep the peace (and both legs) was to compete, grunt like a hero but throw like a wally.

We were allowed two throws each. Darren threw first – a 'no throw'. I was next. I gave it all I had and, grunting loudly enough to raise the dead, I achieved 3 metres 25cm.

'Jaz' laughed and 'accidentally' trod on my foot as he made his way to take his first throw. He steadied himself in the concrete throwing circle, spun round in a professional shot putting style and threw the shot 3 metres 78cm. Phew, thank goodness for that! So far so good; now all I had to do was to muck up my second throw and 'Jaz' would be the winner.

Darren again went first and achieved 3 metres 50cm this time, which drew encouraging but sympathic comments from his watching friends. I picked up the shot, got my balance and hurled the shot. I must have underestimated the benefit of my practice with the neighbour's cat, since my attempt seemed to sail on and on before it thudded to the ground. In actual fact it was only 3 metres 90cm but, what had I done? I told myself not to panic; to stay cool. Surely 'Jaz' could better that; after all his first attempt had nearly got him that far.

He gave me a hard stare, which said all that I needed to know about my fate if he failed to beat me. Picking up the shot he crouched low at the back of the throwing circle – he was obviously going to put every last gram of effort into preserving his reputation. He began to move, spinning quickly on the ball of his right foot. Surely this was to be the winning throw, but, oh disaster, gloom and stress, surely it wasn't. Half way through his super-human effort his foot slipped and in mid-launch he came down in an unco-

The shot slipped from his grasp and nearly flattened the Head's wife.

ordinated heap just outside the throwing circle. The shot slipped from his grasp and nearly flattened the Head's wife who was standing at a safe distance (or so she thought) behind the thrower.

Actually the shot did not flatten her, but 'Jaz's' choice of language did. I'd heard most of the words that 'Jaz' used to express his feelings at his misfortune; the Head's wife hadn't, apparently, since 'Jaz' was immediately dragged off to the Head's office to 'explain himself'.

Now don't ask me why, but ever since that fateful day 'Jaz' has not taken much of a liking to me. Whenever we pass in the corridor he aims a kick at me or tries to take my bag or . . . well, I'm sure you can imagine the situation. Trouble is it might have started as a bit of a joke but it's no joke now – not for me anyway. The prospect of doing battle with 'Jaz' every day is getting more and more depressing. In fact the other day I just couldn't face yet another day of taunts, kicks and bag-snatching so I skived off school. I told my Mum that I had a headache so she let me stay at home. I can't keep on doing that though, can I, so what can I do?

Bible bit

If you are being bullied at the moment you will know how completely hurtful and upsetting it can be. Daily facing threats (and worse) from people who think they can get away with anything, just because they are physically stronger than you, is a miserable way to live. It may be comforting for you to know that God understands EXACTLY how you feel. You see, God has been bullied!

God experienced all the struggles of real life as a human when Jesus (the man who was God) lived on earth 2,000 years ago. OK so there were no school bullies of the 'Jaz' variety, but there were plenty of other sorts about! People with power and authority who didn't like the things that Jesus said and did, and who tried to threaten him or get him beaten up. Eventually they murdered him because they disliked him so much.

One of the biggest bullies at the time was the king, Herod. He didn't care how he got his own way as long as his own way was what he got. There are three important things to learn about bullies from the Bible's description of Herod.

In Mark 6 verses 14–29 you can read the tragic story of Herod ordering the execution of Jesus' cousin, John the Baptist. Herod had arrested John because John kept reminding Herod of how wrong he had been to marry Herodias, who was already married to Herod's brother Philip. Now you may have noticed that bullies don't like having their faults pointed out to them, and so Herod had John locked up in prison. However, Herod did not want to kill John, because, the Bible tells us, 'He was afraid of John because he knew that John was a good and holy man.' Herod could not help but respect John, even as he picked on him. **Bullies are often confused by people who don't fight back but who continue to do what is right.**

A friend of mine had a son called Rick, who was learning brick-laying at a local college. When the other students discovered that he was a Christian they picked on him all the time, frequently ruining his work. He, however, refused to fight back and just kept on doing his best (even though he often went home upset). The bullying got worse and worse until eventually one day the leader of the gang came to him and apologised for being so mean! He explained that he had never met anyone before who didn't fight back. He didn't know how to cope with someone who was nice to him all the time because all the other people that he knew best (including his parents) had always been unkind to him.

Back to Herod, and the second thing to learn from him about bullies. As I've just said, Herod did not intend to kill John the Baptist but his wife, Herodias, did. She hated John, and when Herod rashly promised Herodias' daughter anything she wanted, Herodias made her daughter ask for the head of John the Baptist. Herod, even then, did not have to do it. He could have saved John, but because he didn't want to look soft in front of all the important people who'd heard him promise Herodias' daughter whatever she wanted, Herod killed John as requested.

Herod and all bullies everywhere are basically very weak people who get tough partly to try to hide their weakness. The sort of weakness that I'm talking about is not physical weakness but a weakness of their personality. They are often not very confident (however they may appear) and always want to impress their friends by their unpleasant exploits, so that they feel wanted and accepted by the in-crowd – just like Herod. Being unpleasant is often the only thing they are good at, and so being successful at it makes them feel important. Sad, isn't it, when a human being can only feel good about themselves by being unpleasant to other people?

The third thing that the Bible teaches us about bullies is how to treat them. Herod's still at it, but this time he's feeling worried because so many people keep telling him how wonderful this Jesus person is. Bullies like to be Number One and the thought that someone else could be muscling in on his top-spot got Herod in a bit of a strop. He responded like the true bully that he was – by issuing threats.

> Some Pharisees came to Jesus and said to him, 'You must get out of here and go somewhere else, because Herod wants to kill you' (Luke 13:31).

Now Jesus knew that Herod had killed John and that therefore this might be no empty threat. But this is how Jesus responds:

> 'Go and tell that fox: "I am driving out demons and performing cures today and tomorrow, and on the third day I shall finish my work!" ' (Luke 13:32).

In other words: 'Go chase yourself, Herod. I'm going to keep doing what is right and no threats from you are going to stop me!' Although this route is tough, it is the only way to stop the bully. **If you give in to bullying and threats then the bully wins and 'Wrong' has defeated 'Right'.** Maybe at this point we ought to get on to some. . . .

Practical pointers and handy hints

1   Whatever may have been threatened or done, do not give in to the bully and do not keep whatever has happened to yourself. Tell a trusted friend – preferably an adult – and ask them for advice about what to do.

2   If hurtful things have been said to you or about you don't let your mind keep going over and over them. Again, explain what's been said to a close friend and

keep reminding yourself that in God's eyes you are a successful, important and useful person. (See chapter 2 – 'A testing time'.)

3 If things get really bad you MUST tell your parent(s) and one of your teachers. If any of your friends are aware of what has been happening, take them with you.

4 Do everything that YOU can to avoid making matters worse. 'Do everything possible on your part to live in peace with everybody' (Romans 12:18). Don't deliberately stir up trouble.

5 Pray for the person that is picking on you. Ask God to use you to change that person for the better. And 'ask God to bless those who persecute you – yes, ask him to bless, not to curse' (Romans 12:14).

6 'If someone has done you wrong, do not repay him with a wrong. Try to do what everyone considers to be good' (Romans 12:17). As we've already seen, the average bully can't cope with people who don't fight or answer back.

7 Walking away from a potentially ugly situation is not failure. Jesus did it (Luke 4: 28–30) so it must make sense!

Think about it
1 In the space below write in your own words one thing that you have learned which has helped you understand bullies better.

2 Write the names of anyone who you know is a bully or anyone who is being bullied. How can you help them?

Damnation Derek

School playgrounds are supposed to be safe places, and in general I suppose that they are. In my experience very few genuine disasters ever happen in the school playground. For example:

1. I have never seen anyone eaten by crocodiles.
2. I have never seen anyone flattened by a runaway horse and cart.
3. I have never seen anyone drown in a lake of boiling marmalade and . . .
4. I have never seen anyone fall down a disused mine shaft.

I could go on, but this is enough to prove my initial statement that there is a sort of safety to be found in your average school playground. However, this safety is sometimes a fairly flimsy thing.

It is true that the perils associated with the school playground are of a different order to those listed above, but none the less perils there are. Here is my 'List of Potential Playground Perils':

1. Small pupils attempting to run between the legs of larger pupils playing football.
2. Larger pupils attempting to step over smaller pupils playing football.
3. Large pupils playing netball with smaller pupils (as opposed to with a ball).
4. 'Jaz', 'Daz' and 'Maz'. (See the first chapter, 'With friends like those'!)
5. Playing 'catch' with crisp bags full of water.
6. Opening the can of Coke that has been rattling round in your school bag all morning.

Health warning! Perils 5 and 6 are especially dangerous if performed too near the member of staff on duty.

7. 'Damnation Derek'.

I reckon that you can all understand Perils 1 – 6 because they (or something very like them) are pretty common to all school playgrounds. However, Peril number 7 maybe needs some explanation because it is possible that you have never encountered a 'Damnation Derek'.

'Damnation Derek' is not strictly speaking a 'Peril', he is a person of the large, Year 12 variety. He is, furthermore, a Christian and a member of the school Christian Union (room 19 – Friday lunch-time). Now 'Damnation Derek' is not one of your wimpy-never-let-anyone-know-that-you-go-to-church type of Christians, he is the sort of Christian that doesn't mind who knows that he goes to church, believes in God, reads the Bible and prays (etc, etc). In fact, 'Damnation Derek' is a Christian who believes in 'Witnessing' and it is this simple, even commendable desire to tell others about God and all things Christian that has earned him his nickname ('Damnation' isn't his real name – in case you thought he had very unloving parents!) and which has made him a Playground Health Hazard.

Each morning break-time 'Damnation Derek' can be seen – and heard – 'Witnessing' in the playground. His tactics are simple enough. He arrives on the scene about two minutes after the bell has rung for the start of break, clutching his large black Bible under his arm. He will pause briefly to survey the assembled masses and select a victim – usually a small, isolated Year Niner. 'Damnation' will approach his target and introduce himself with an opening line which usually goes something like, 'Hi. If you fell from the top of the ropes in the sports hall this afternoon would you go to heaven or hell?' You see, 'Damnation' likes to be loving and tactful when he first meets someone!

The small Year Niner usually looks a bit blank – possibly because she has never considered the possibility of either heaven OR hell lying at the foot of the ropes in the sports hall – and responds with a vague, 'Uh?'

Undaunted 'Damnation' takes this response as encouragement to continue his 'Witnessing' and attempts to clarify the situation by asking, 'Are you covered by the blood of Jesus?'

'Damnation' likes to be loving and tactful when he first meets someone!

Light dawns on the small Year Niner's face as she hastens to explain that the stain on the front of her school blouse is jam that has squirted out of her break-time doughnut, and not blood at all.

'Damnation' now makes his final contribution to the salvation of this small Year Niner's soul by explaining that 'streams of living water can be found in room 19 any Friday lunch-time for those who are thirsty enough to seek it.' The small Year

Niner, who did not even realise that there were taps in room 19, never mind streams, is a little interested by this offer but explains that her Mum never lets her drink the water at school and always provides her with a carton of fruit juice which keeps her going through the day.

'Damnation' now feels good that this small Year Niner has been 'Witnessed' to and moves on to his next victim. Not much of a 'Peril' maybe, but if you see him moving in your direction I suggest that you start moving in the opposite one. (Alternatively, you could pretend that you have just been beamed down from outer space and that you do not understand a word that he is saying – which is at least partly true!)

Bible bit

The Bible does have quite a bit to say about Christians – all Christians – being witnesses for Jesus, BUT it does not have very much at all to say about the sort of 'Witnessing' being done by 'Damnation Derek'. A good Bible passage to look at to understand real Christian witnessing is 1 Peter 3:14–16.

> Do not be afraid of anyone and do not worry. But have reverence for Christ in your hearts, and honour him as Lord. Be ready at all times to answer anyone who asks you to explain the hope you have in you, but do it with gentleness and respect. Keep your conscience clear so that when you are insulted, those who speak evil of your good conduct as followers of Christ will be ashamed of what they say.

These verses mention six important things about telling others about Jesus:

1 'Do not be afraid of anyone but have reverence for Christ.' This was about the only thing that 'Damnation Derek' got right! He certainly wasn't afraid of what people thought of him! Sometimes, though, we can be so afraid of what other people think that we shut up rather than speak up. What do you really think is more important, disappointing your 'friends' by 'going all religious on them' or disappointing Jesus by failing to stand up for him? If your friends really cared about their friendship with you they wouldn't mock your beliefs.

2 'Be ready to answer . . .' Probably if 'Damnation Derek' had bothered to talk to people and get to know them a bit before preaching at them, he would have discovered that they would want to ask him some questions about what he believed. When you meet someone who cares deeply about something, you probably will want to ask them questions about why they care so much. If your true friends know that you are a Christian, sooner or later they will want to know something about your faith. 'What's your church like?' 'Isn't the Bible heavy-duty reading?' 'How can Jesus be alive today if he died 2,000 years ago?' etc, etc. Real witnessing is more about answering friends' questions than telling strangers things that they are not interested in.

3 'Be ready . . . to explain.' This is where so many Christians come off the rails. They quite simply cannot explain WHY they believe WHAT they believe, and so rather than admit their ignorance about their own faith, they just shut up. For instance you probably know that Christians believe that Jesus came alive again after being dead and buried for three days. But WHY do we believe that? Are there good reasons to believe it?

Isn't there a better explanation for Jesus' body disappearing from the grave?

You also know that Christians base everything that they believe on what the Bible says. But again, WHY? Is every word in the Bible really straight from the mouth of God? Hasn't it been changed over the years to say different things from what the original writers intended? This is a REALLY IMPORTANT question, because if we cannot believe the Bible then we can just believe what we like (as most people who don't have much of a faith do) and reject what we don't like.

I hope that you are beginning to see why it's important for you to be able to explain what you believe and why you believe it. This requires you to do a bit of work. Spend a bit of time at your local Christian bookshop looking at books that help you find the answers to your questions. Keep pestering your parents (if they are Christians), or your church leader or youth leader for answers, and listen carefully to what they say.

A final word of warning on this point – don't be disappointed if the answer has to be, 'I don't know.' There are some things that God has not told us, and therefore we do not know. For example, we do not know exactly how God made the world, but that doesn't stop us believing that he DID make the world. Non-Christians (if they are honest) have to say that they don't know how the world and life was made; they've got loads of ideas (which they call 'theories') but they do not and cannot KNOW. All they can do is to look at the evidence and decide what they are going to believe. Looking at the evidence leads many scientists to believe that God made the world, whereas other scientists look at the same evidence and believe that it all happened by chance and that the world, the solar system, you and me are all just the result of a lucky string of enormous flukes!

4 'Do it with gentleness and respect.' Witnessing is not ramming your opinions and beliefs down someone else's ear trumpet but gently explaining what you believe. Witnessing should never become an excuse for a heated argument; if things are moving in that direction it's better to end the conversation sooner rather than later. You can always respect someone else's viewpoint without necessarily agreeing with it.

5 'Keep your conscience clear.' There are no guarantees that people will believe what you believe about God, Jesus, the Bible etc. (That does not, of course, mean that they are right and you are wrong!)

However, one thing that is almost guaranteed is that if the things that you do don't match up to the things that you say, your friends will soon point that out to you!

If you talk about believing the Bible to be true and then go out and pick on someone who you don't get on with, your friends may remind you that the Bible has something to say about Christians loving their enemies! Witnessing is as much about showing people Christianity in the way we live as it is about explaining Christianity by the things that we say. (More on this in the next chapter.)

6 Be prepared to be insulted. You know and I know that not everyone will agree with you. This is usually because they've never thought much about Christianity and the only opinions that they have got are ones that they've picked up from their parent(s) or the TV. (Have you noticed how the Christians on TV are usually the 'wet' ones, like Harold in Neighbours – it's no wonder that people think ALL Christians are wet!) So, when you start talking about Christianity or church or the Bible, probably the only answers that your friends have got are based on what they've heard from others, like 'It's all just made up,' or, 'Jesus never really existed.'

If you then try to ask them WHY they believe that 'it's all made up' they won't have the foggiest idea and may get a bit abusive and say things like, 'Only wallies believe that load of junk.' All they are doing is trying to hide their own ignorance about Jesus and the Bible by being rude to you!

Being insulted occasionally is all part of the package deal with real witnessing – no witness, no insult.

Practical pointers and handy hints

1 Never imagine that one day it'll be really easy to witness. It DOES get easier, but the longer you keep your mouth shut about Jesus the harder it becomes to speak out.

2 Write down all the difficult questions that you don't feel you have an answer for and try to find a person or a book that helps you answer them.

3 Pray every day that God will fill you with the Holy Spirit so that you have more courage to speak up for Jesus.

4 Never feel a failure if you have to admit that you don't know the answer to a friend's question. It's better to admit that you don't know and then go away to find out the answer, than to make up an answer that is not true!

5 Don't get drawn into pointless arguments. Try to learn to tell the difference between people who are just wanting to have a row and people who REALLY want to know more about Jesus.

6 If you have a good Christian friend, you could always practise witnessing by one of you pretending to be an interested non-Christian and the other being her/himself. The one who is 'playing' the role of the non-Christian should ask all the usual questions that your friends may ask, and the one who is being the Christian should attempt to answer. After a few questions and answers swap roles, and then discuss how convincing the Christian's answers were to the non-Christian.

7 Don't believe that you have to understand everything about Christianity before you can start explaining what you believe to your friends. Start with what you DO know – nobody understands everything!

Think about it

1 Write down the name of one friend who you think may be interested in knowing a bit more about what you believe as a Christian. Pray for an opportunity to speak to them (and then look out for the opportunity during the week).

2 Which do you care about more – keeping in with your friends or keeping in with Jesus?

Loving the Jesus way

I don't think I've told you about Mr Grovey our drama teacher yet, have I? We all call him Mr Groovy – which he isn't, but it usually gets a laugh. (From the rest of the class, not from Mr Grovey.)

Mr Grovey is very thin. He has a bald head and a long beard, the combined effect of which is to make it appear as though his head is stuck on upside down. Like all teachers, he uses the phrase 'Right then' all the time. ('Right then, quieten down', 'Right then, let's see that group's work', 'Right then, who turned the lights off?' etc, etc.) He is actually a very good drama teacher, and because ALL drama lessons are practical they make a welcome change from the routines of writing, reading and watching videos which are the usual diet in most other subjects.

Mr Grovey likes to appear cool and trendy (as do most teachers under thirty), but for Mr Grovey the attempt at an up-to-date image is ruined by his liking for wearing highly patterned, sleeveless pullovers of the sort seen hanging in charity shops the length and breadth of Britain.

Anyway, in order to get our interest at the start of each lesson he usually involves us in a silly game of some sort, and I still clearly remember the drama lesson when, thanks to David Smith (alias 'Daz'), the 'warm up' game went horribly wrong.

The instructions were clear enough. 'Right then, we'll start with a concentration exercise.' (Posh name for silly game!) 'Right then,' Mr Grovey bellowed, 'I'll call out an instruction like this; "Let's all hop on one leg," OK? Whenever an instruction starts with the words "Let's all" everyone MUST do it. But if I just say, "Hop on one leg," you should ignore the instruction. All clear? Right then, "Let's all touch all four walls of the drama studio." '

Immediately everyone charged around the room attempting to be the first to touch all the walls. 'Right then, sit down.' A few people sat on the floor (no chairs in the drama studio) and jumped straight to their feet again as an outbreak of jeering laughter told them that they'd got it wrong. And so the game, er . . . exercise, continued until Mr Grovey ran out of ideas AND made his big mistake at one and the same time.

'Right then, I've called out enough instructions, now I'll point to one of you and you must make up the instruction to be obeyed in just the same way as I have been doing. All right?' It was all right, so he pointed at Darren, who after a moment's thought said, 'Let's all take our shoes off' – which we did, amidst much good humoured nose-holding. So far so good, but Mr Grovey then pointed at David Smith ('Daz'), who without the need for any thought whatever said, 'Let's all throw our shoes at Mr Grovey.' There was only the slightest of pauses for communal reflection before twenty-nine pairs of shoes were duly launched at the teacher in charge.

Twenty-nine pairs of shoes were launched at the teacher in charge.

To say that Mr Grovey was not amused is a bit of an understatement. I have rarely, if ever, seen a teacher whose flabber was so gasted. I won't bore you with the details of what happened next but the exercise was over and so was 'Daz's' participation in the lesson. He spent the rest of the double period seated at a desk in the corridor copying chunks of Shakespeare plays onto pieces of file paper.

After a suitably stern telling off from Mr Grovey (whose bald head always got redder the angrier he got) the lesson moved on to the next phase. 'Right then, get into pairs, please.' A simple enough request, you might think, but one that always caused complaint and argument.

The reason for the complaint was that given the even numbers in the class (now that 'Daz' was in the corridor!), someone now had to work with Brian Smart. The reason for the argument was that no one wanted to. It wasn't Brian's fault; he couldn't really help the fact that he didn't fit in, that he looked, well . . . strange, or that he was at the back of the queue when the brains were handed out. Nobody ever volunteered to work with Brian, so Mr Grovey always had to force someone to, usually by threatening something terrible if they refused.

As Mr Grovey searched the room for a suitable candidate to partner Brian this week, unhappily his eye fell on me (not literally of course, it's just a way of saying 'he looked at me'!). My heart sank (again, not literally!) as I heard him say, 'Right then, I'm sure you'll work with Brian today, won't you David?'

Bible bit
If you had to fill in the gap at the end of the following sentence, what would you put? Have a go.

Being a Christian is all about learning to ....

OK. How did you complete the sentence? No points if you wrote:

'eat spaghetti with chop-sticks,'

or

'juggle soot blindfolded.'

Two points if you mentioned praying, reading the Bible, knowing God or anything along those lines, but for the purposes of this chapter you get a score of 5 . . . yes, 5 points, if you mentioned respecting and caring for other people.

As I mentioned in the chapter on 'Teachers', the Bible has got a lot of things to say about how we get on with other people. It keeps using this word, LOVE. In fact if one thing marks out a Christian as being different it should be this thing called 'love'. Not the sort of love that you see in films when the big hairy hero takes his girlfriend in his arms, half suffocates her with a big slobbering kiss and then says, 'I love you, Ermentrude.' No, when you read the word 'love' in the Bible it means something completely different; you don't have to hug anyone, kiss anyone or call them Ermentrude to love them the Jesus way.

The first thing to learn about Jesus' love is that it's available to everybody twenty-four hours a day; it's not only for wealthy, good-looking brain-boxes. In fact the people who Jesus chose to spend time with, to care for and even to heal were not the 'successful' people of his day but the Brian Smarts of his day. People like Zacchaeus for example.

OK, so Zacchaeus was clever, but that was about

all he had going for him. He was short and deeply unpopular with everyone because he had cheated them out of their money when he collected their taxes for the Roman army. Even Mr Grovey would never have got anyone to work in a pair with Zacchaeus!

Now Jesus came to town one day and everyone – including Zacchaeus – wanted to get a look at this healer who they'd heard so much about. Zacchaeus knew he wouldn't get a very good look at Jesus because he was too short to see over the heads of the crowd, so he shinned up a tree. All went according to plan and as Jesus came into view Zacchaeus could see him clearly. He was a bit disappointed actually; Jesus looked so ordinary.

But just as Jesus and the following crowd passed under Zacchaeus' perch, Jesus stopped and looked straight up at him. Zacchaeus' heart missed a beat as all the crowd started telling Jesus who he was, and how he'd regularly cheated them out of their money. They told Jesus how he was getting richer and richer as they got poorer and poorer, and how he didn't have any pity even on people who really couldn't afford to pay.

Zacchaeus gritted his teeth and waited for a great long telling off from Jesus. He'd heard how Jesus was always concerned for poor people and how he always welcomed the chance to correct people like him who were living wrongly. But . . . what was Jesus saying? Zacchaeus could hardly hear because of the row the crowd was making. Yes, this time he did hear, 'Hurry down, Zacchaeus, because I must stay in your house today!'

Oh, wow! Jesus having tea at the home of a cheating thief!! Whatever next? But this is the whole point about Jesus' love – it went out to everyone. Jesus said if someone is another Christian – love them. If someone is a friend – love them. If someone is an enemy – love them. If someone is a lonely cheat stuck up a tree – love them. If someone is a 'Brian Smart' (and you've got them in your school) – love them. You don't have to LIKE the things that they do or say to LOVE them; Jesus certainly didn't like Zacchaeus' cheating, but he loved Zacchaeus!

Just stop and think about this a minute. If Jesus had been in your class for drama, who would he have chosen to work with in a pair?

Loving the Jesus way is explained a lot more fully in the Bible, in 1 Corinthians 13:1–8.

I may be able to speak the languages of men and even of angels, but if I have no love my speech is no more than a noisy gong or a clanging bell. I may have the gift of inspired preaching; I may have all knowledge and understand all secrets; I may have all the faith needed to move mountains – but if I have no love, I am nothing. I may give away everything I have, and even give up my body to be burned – but if I have no love this does me no good.

Love is patient and kind; it is not jealous or con-ceited or proud; love is not ill-mannered or selfish or irritable; love does not keep a record or wrongs; love is not happy with evil but is happy with the truth. Love never gives up; and its faith, hope and patience never fail.

So let's just use this passage to make a Loving The Jesus Way At School checklist. See how you get on.

1. I am patient with the Brian Smarts of this world. **Y/N**

2. I am kind to the people at school that others laugh at. **Y/N**

3. I am not jealous of people who do things better than I can. **Y/N**

4. I don't have to boast about things that I do well. **Y/N**

5. I am not ill-mannered, even to unpopular teachers! **Y/N**

6. I am prepared to share my possessions with people who have less than I do. **Y/N**

7. I am willing to forgive people who have upset me and do not bear grudges against them. **Y/N**

8. I am not happy when something unfair happens to someone else and I try to stand up for what is right. **Y/N**

9. I never give up on people – even those who have let me down in the past. **Y/N**

Well, how did you get on? If you're like me you've still got a fair way to go! But don't let your failures put you off trying harder. Just think how much of a better place school would be if EVERYONE loved the Jesus way! No more arguing. No more people left out and laughed at for being different. No more hurtful comments about people's looks. Of course it is extremely unlikely that EVERYONE will start loving the Jesus way, but that's no reason why YOU shouldn't start. Here to get you started are a few. . . .

Practical pointers and handy hints

1 Think about your class and year group. Who are the people without many friends? Aim to be a better friend to just one of them, starting from today!

2 When your class moves from lesson to lesson, look out for anyone walking on their own and walk with them.

3 When other people are taking the mickey out of someone else, try to imagine how they feel about it. Don't join in if it is getting hurtful.

4 Be prepared to be the first one to stand up for what is right when something wrong is being done to or said about someone.

5 Remember Jesus' Golden Rule: 'Do to others just what you want them to do for you.'

6 If your class is told to divide into groups by the teacher, keep a look-out for people who are not in a group and invite them into yours.

7 Lunch-times can go on for ever if you have no friends and no one invites you to join in with what they are doing. Look out for anyone standing around on their own, and if possible try to involve them in what you are doing.

Think about it

1 Make a list of words that describe how you think Brian Smart would feel about coming to school each day.

2 Write down a prayer for any 'Brian Smarts' known to you.

Belinda Buckle fancies you

The news came as a complete surprise. Belinda Buckle? Me? Surely there must be some mistake! Whatever could Belinda Buckle see in me? Perhaps the messenger had delivered the information to the wrong person. Maybe it was intended for Darren White or even Richard Morrison . . . but not me.

I certainly wanted it to be true because I was the only boy (well, nearly the only boy) in our class never to have had a girlfriend and I was beginning to feel a bit left out. But what should I do now that I'd been told about Belinda's feelings? There were several options that occurred to me:

1. Go to find her at lunch-time, throw my arms round her and promise my never-ending life-long devotion.
2. Slip a notice into the Head's assembly announcements, asking her to marry me.

3. Quietly pass her a note in our next lesson asking if I could sit next to her on the bus on the way home tonight.

I sat and pondered these options for some time before deciding that numbers 1 and 2 were probably a bit over the top (especially if it WAS Darren White that she really fancied!). Plan 3 it was then. Right, now what to put in the note?

How should I begin? 'Dear Belinda' er . . . 'Dearest Belinda' er . . . , no, I know, Belinda's

Whatever could Belinda Buckle see in me?

into poetry; it'd really impress her if I made my note into a poem! It took several attempts to get it right, but in the end I felt justifiably proud of my literary effort.

My fairest BB
From you to me
A message came today

Did I get it right
Or was it for D White?
'For me,' oh do please say.

I like your long hair
It touches the chair
Of you I would make a fuss

If you want to hold hands
Or flick elastic bands
Sit next to me on the school bus (tonight).

Poem by DL for BB

(In all honesty I didn't really think that she would want to flick elastic bands but I couldn't think of what else to rhyme with 'hands'.) Apart from that, I had said more or less what I wanted to say in a way that I thought Belinda could not fail to admire. The next problem was how to deliver it, since I sat at the back in English (our next lesson) and Belinda sat at the front – which was how I knew that her hair touched her chair!

The lesson had started and I still didn't know how to deliver my masterpiece. I considered simply passing it forward, but some idiot would probably open it and read it out to the whole class, or else it would get intercepted by Mrs Burton who was the last person that I wanted to read it. No, somehow I had to cut out the middle-men and middle-women. My final solution to the problem was a bit risky, but not as risky as the alternatives – or so I thought!

I was readily acknowledged as the Class Paper Aeroplane Making Champion (once constructing a complicated four-wing design which flew 12 metres in a dead straight line) and so I decided to put my skills to good use. Folding the sheet containing the poem into what I hoped was the perfect paper 'plane, I waited until Mrs Burton's back was turned and I launched the message-bearing missile in Belinda's direction. It flew dead straight, and was just about to begin its descent towards Belinda's desk when Jason Drew, who was sitting immediately behind Belinda, put his hand up to ask a question. The 'plane hit his raised arm which deflected its flight path, onto the desk of Rebecca Bradshaw.

Rebecca (or 'Becky' as everyone calls her) picked up the plane and, noticing that there was writing on it, slowly unfolded it. There was a slight delay as she read it and then her head slowly turned in my direction and she gave me the biggest grin I'd ever seen. What was going on? Oh no . . . light slowly dawned. 'Becky Bradshaw' . . . 'BB' . . . .

My brain began to overheat at the sheer scale of the disaster that had just overtaken me. Becky thought that she was the 'BB' whose hand I wanted to hold on the bus tonight. Aaargh!! To be fair, Becky was all right – in her way – but she was no Belinda. Belinda was fun, lively, and good looking. Becky was, well, sort of ordinary if you know what I mean. Oh grief, pain and stress – what was I going to do?

Bible bit

The Bible doesn't have a great deal to say about boys and girls going out with girls and boys. People officially became adults at the age of twelve in Bible times, and at that age, or shortly after, their parents arranged who they would marry! The Jewish law expected a boy to get married between the age of thirteen and eighteen to a Jewish girl aged twelve-and-a-half to fifteen!! You can see that there's no point in the Bible writers wasting ink explaining how to go out with someone who fancies you when 'going out' and 'fancying' weren't part of the way that they did things then!

HOWEVER, the Bible does have a load of things to say about how to treat other people and about how to build friendships. A lot of this good advice is easy to apply to girl/boy relationships. Here are a few 'Bible Bits' to help you understand friendships a bit better:

1 'Good looks or trendy clothes can be misleading. What's really important is whether or not someone loves God' (my version of Proverbs 31:30).

The Bible is quite clear that it is always a mistake for a Christian to go out with a non-Christian. Sooner or later (and it'll probably be sooner) your different beliefs will come between you.

2 'Beauty is only skin-deep. What's really important is the sort of person you are' (my version of 1 Peter 3:4).

TV programmes, adverts and magazines always show a certain sort of person as attractive. There's a certain shape that's shown as the 'right way' to look – usually slim for girls and tall and broad-shouldered for guys! There are certain sorts of clothes that make you an 'OK person' (like Levi jeans or Reebok trainers).

There's an old saying that goes 'you should never judge a book by its cover', and I would say 'you should never judge a person by their looks.' Deciding that you want to go out with someone because they happen to fit into this year's idea of what is good looking is stupid. The Bible's right (surprise, surprise), you should always try to get to know what a person is really like before deciding whether or not you want to build a deep friendship with them.

3 'You must not be envious of your friends'. . . .

So begins the last of the Ten Commandments (Exodus 20:17). It's always a great temptation to look around, see what other people are doing or what they have got and want to be like them. In the story above, David says that he's the only boy in his class who's not been out with a girl. Now that's probably not really true – it just seems that way to him! But my point is that whether it's true or not doesn't matter. We are us, you are you, I am me and our friends are our friends! What they do is up to them and you shouldn't feel that you have to copy them. It's not wrong or odd to be different, in fact it's far wiser to think things out for yourself than just to blindly and unthinkingly follow the crowd.

If everyone else has got boy or girl friends, so what? No one says that YOU have to, and if your main reason for wanting a close friendship is to be like everyone else then it won't be much of a friendship anyway!

4 'Respect everyone' (1 Peter 2:17).

One of the words that the Bible uses most often to describe a Christian's relationships is this word 'respect'. What does it mean to 'respect' someone? The Concise Oxford Dictionary (which I'm sure you read every night before going to sleep) says that if you respect someone you will avoid:
– degrading them (putting them down)
– insulting them
– injuring them
– offending them
– tempting them
– corrupting them.

It also says that if you respect someone you will 'treat them with consideration' and 'esteem them' (think of them as valuable).

All relationships should be built on respect but, perhaps especially, close friendships should be especially respectful! Just wanting to go out with someone because they 'fancy you' or because you 'fancy them' just isn't enough. Do you really care for them? Do you really respect them?

5 'Don't be selfish; don't live to make a good impression on others' (Philippians 2:3 in the Living Bible).

What is your real reason for wanting to go out with that person? It's always wrong to want a special friendship with someone just so that you feel better about yourself or so that others are impressed.

6 'Don't just think about your own affairs, but be

interested in others too' (Philippians 2:4 in the Living Bible).

Even when you do start going out with someone special, don't spend ALL your time with them. Keep good friendships with everyone. If you and your girl/boyfriend are at youth group – talk to other people and take part in the activities. It makes things awkward for everyone if you both act like someone has super-glued you together.

Practical pointers and handy hints

1 Don't feel a failure if you've never had a boyfriend or girlfriend. It doesn't make you odd and doesn't mean that you never will. Be patient, your time will come!

2 Be a good friend to as many people as possible – boys and girls.

3 Never judge someone by the way they look.

4 Sometimes close friendships can go wrong or get a bit hurtful. Try to find an adult (parent, youth leader, etc) who you trust enough to be able to talk to about all of your friendships. It's important that you're pre-pared to listen to their advice too!

5 Never look at other people as 'things' to own for a while and then dump when you're fed up with them. People of whatever shape and size are all created and loved by God and all deserve respect (see above).

6 Don't be conned by your school friends or by what you see on TV! The most important part of boy/girl relationships is NOT holding hands, cuddling and kiss-ing! In fact as I've said above that's really the least important part. Friendship is about caring for the other person, respecting the other person, sharing your interests with the other person, enjoying just being with the other person – but not about suffocating the other person with big slobbering kisses!

Think about it

1 What do you think the difficulties could be if a Christian went out with a non-Christian?

2 Create your own acrostic on the word RESPECT. Each new word or phrase across should be something that you consider important in building good relationships with others. (I've filled in a couple to get you started.)

R

Enjoying being together

S

P

E

C

Trust

Just a game?

I don't know whether you realise this or not, but your school has a prospectus. A prospectus is a sort of handbook which is supposed to tell you and your parents everything that you need to know about surviving at your school. I say 'supposed to tell you', because there are always important bits of information missed out of the school prospectus; for example, they never tell you that,

'No loo door in this school has a lock,'

or,

'A recording of the school's brass band is used in place of warning sirens on all local police vehicles.'

No, nothing so useful or interesting is ever included. Instead the average school prospectus is usually full of statements like this:

'Every pupil at Kidminster Green is cared for by a personal tutor who remains with the tutor group throughout the pupil's school career. At the start of each school day there is a twenty minute tutorial time, during which personal, social and moral values are discussed within the tutor group.'

Personally I think whoever wrote the prospectus of Kidminster Green should be taken to court and charged with 'Gross Deceit of Parents and Pupils' because what actually takes place in the first twenty minutes of the school day bears absolutely no relation to what the prospectus claims should happen. Bearing the above statement in mind, take my tutor group as a fairly typical example of the point that I'm trying to make.

The bell rings at 8.45 and we all gather at the door to our tutor base. Actually it would be more accurate to call it a tutor 'hut' since our class is based in one of those 'temporary' classrooms that sprouted up around schools all over the country about twenty years ago. Ours hasn't been decorated since it was erected because every year is supposed to be its 'last' year. A few half-hearted attempts at brightening the place up with posters have been made by a succession of teachers, but it doesn't really help because the huts suffer from terminal damp and the posters quickly go all brown and blotchy making the general appearance of the hut's interior more, not less, gloomy.

We usually have to queue up in the rain because Mr Barnes – our 'Supa-Tuta' – keeps the door locked until his arrival, to prevent vandalism (although there are those who think that a spot of creative vandalism would smarten the place up a bit!). He arrives without the key and sends a runner to the office to retrieve it, while he calls the register in the rain.

The runner soon returns and we all shuffle soggily into the hut. Mr Barnes usually then says something like, 'Right then, get on with something useful. I've got a lot of preparation to do before first period.' At this point it is really interesting to note the variety of activities that the members of my class regard as 'useful'. Here are a sample few:

1. Copying last night's homework from the class 'mega-brain'.
2. Staring out of the window.
3. Cleaning dirty fingernails with straightened out paper clips.
4. Writing 'DF 4 SM' on the back of your hand.
5. Hiding Brian Smart's bag in the stock cupboard.
6. Eating your packed lunch.
7. Hiding Brian Smart's coat in the stock cupboard.
8. Seeing how red you can go by holding your breath.
9. Hiding Brian Smart in the stock cupboard.
10. Picking your nose.

Now I suppose some of these ARE useful (although I'm not sure which ones) but I am sure that none of them help develop my 'personal, moral and social values' as claimed by the school prospectus.

The variety of activities that my class regard as 'useful'.

To be fair there was a week when Mr Barnes spotted this inconsistency too and suggested that seeing as how we all wasted our tutor time (WE wasted it – I like that!) we should bring in a board game next week and he'd organise a sort of tournament.

Well several people did bring in board games but Mr Barnes was 'too busy' to organise us, so we just joined in with whatever we fancied. Some played Monopoly (which is a daft game to try to play in twenty minutes – even my Mum couldn't go bankrupt in that time) and others joined several games together and invented one new one which they called 'Scruvial Cluedopolybats'.

There was one small group though who went through to the store area at the back of the hut and got on with something really quietly. I thought that they were cribbing up last night's French homework but it turns out that they were playing a game called 'Ouija'. Apparently they all had to sit in a circle and put their hands on the playing board. They then asked the board questions and a pointer on the board moved to either 'yes' or 'no' to give them an answer. The girls that were using it reckoned that they were contacting 'the spirit world' but I reckoned it was all a big con trick. Anyway, whatever, it got pretty popular for a bit before everyone got bored with it and went back to staring out of the window and hiding Brian Smart (and his accessories) in the stock cupboard.

So that's tutor time at Kidminster Green; so much for the school prospectus eh?

Bible bit

'Games' like Ouija are not really games at all. They really do try to contact the invisible 'spirit world' that surrounds us all.

Many people today only believe in what they can see and touch and so they don't believe in spirits, demons, angels or even God! (Despite what they may say, everyone DOES believe in invisible things – no one doubts the existence of wind, electricity, love or toothache, even though no one has ever seen any of those things!)

Anyway, the important thing is not whether people

believe in something or not – the important thing is whether it's actually true or not. I might really believe that smoking cigarettes does me no harm. I might ignore all the warnings and even try to convince other people that lung cancer does not really exist. The point is that whether I believe it or not, and whether I convince my friends that I'm right or not, does not alter the fact that smoking cigarettes causes lung cancer.

In just the same way a lot of your friends may choose not to believe in God . . . or Jesus . . . or angels . . . or evil spirits, and they may even try to convince you that they are right! But are they?

As far as the Bible is concerned there is very definitely a real but invisible 'spirit world' which surrounds us all. The Bible is quite clear that God is a spirit and that he commands an action force of good spirits (usually called angels).

But the 'spirit world' also has its baddies. God has an invisible enemy, Satan, who, although very evil, is greatly inferior to God. Satan also commands a spirit action force; an evil one of 'demons' and 'evil spirits'.

The Bible is quite clear that these evil spirits (and the things that they do) are dangerous. It warns us that we should not have anything to do with them or with people who try to use their powers.

Activities like 'Ouija' really are trying to contact spiritual powers – but the power comes from evil spirits not God's spirits. Evil spiritual powers; let's look at that name more closely:

EVIL – because they are only interested in damaging our lives, not in helping us.

SPIRITUAL – because they are not people; they are real invisible beings, or spirits.

POWERS – because IF WE LET THEM they really DO have the power to hurt us and damage our lives.

So how can these evil spiritual powers affect our lives? These powers are very crafty and will look for any opportunity to get at us. If we get involved in activities which claim to contact hidden powers (another word for 'hidden' is 'occult') – then, often without meaning to, we open our minds to those harmful influences.

Remember that anything that claims to work by means of spiritual powers needs to be looked at carefully. There are only two sources of spiritual power: God and Satan. Every invisible spirit is either on God's side or on Satan's side.

Lots of activities that need a spiritual power to make them work are actually outlawed by God in the Bible, so any spiritual power being used in them is clearly not from him but is from Satan; God wouldn't ban something that he'd created for our good!

The sorts of activities that the Bible warns us against would include:

– ouija boards
– astrology (horoscopes)
– mind reading
– levitation
– palm reading
– tarot cards
– séances

You may not have heard of some of these things, but one day you probably will. Just remember that the invisible spiritual force that makes them work is evil and harmful, so leave them all well alone.

We may not understand the occult (hidden) powers

that lie behind these activities but be warned – they are REAL and they are HARMFUL.

Take, for example, the true story of John:

John was invited by some friends to 'play' with a ouija board. He'd never done it before but thought it sounded like harmless fun.

During the 'game', the board predicted the death of the best friend of someone taking part.

John thought no more about it – until, two weeks later, HIS best friend was killed in a freak motorcycle accident.

During the months that followed, John's life was miserable. He blamed himself for the death of his friend, thinking that if he hadn't used the ouija board, perhaps his friend would still be alive.

At times John felt like taking his own life as a kind of token repayment for the life of his friend.

Satan was delighted to cause John so much guilt and misery. Satan is interested in bringing misery . . . suffering . . . pain . . . and guilt into our lives. Think about it! You don't want to run the risk of someone like that getting at you, so steer right away from any of the sorts of activities listed above.

Practical pointers and handy hints

1 If you have never been involved in any of the activities listed above then DON'T . . . DON'T . . . DON'T!! Even if your friends urge you to join in . . . DON'T . . . DON'T . . . DON'T!!

2 Don't be frightened of evil spirits. They cannot just choose to hurt you, you have to give them the chance (for example by joining in activities like those listed above) – so don't!

3 If you have been involved in any occult activities in the past then DON'T PANIC, just read on.

4 Although Satan has the power to hurt people who get too close to him, his power is not unstoppable! Jesus Christ has the power to destroy all the harmful effects of what Satan tries to do. This is what the Bible has to say on the subject:

> The Son of God [Jesus] appeared for this very reason, to destroy what the devil [Satan] had done (1 John 3:8).

> If the Son [Jesus] sets you free, you will be free indeed (John 8:34).

5 If you want a clean start, Jesus can give it to you! He can replace the negative influence of Satan with the positive power of God's Holy Spirit. So . . .

6 Pray to Jesus. Tell him how sorry you are for letting Satan influence your life. Ask him to 'throw out' anything harmful which may be affecting you.

7 Ask Jesus to fill your mind and spirit with his Holy Spirit.

8 Talk to an older Christian about your experiences. Show them this chapter of the book and ask them to pray with you. Ask for their advice about how to stay close to Jesus. This may seem like a hard thing to do, but if you've been involved with occult powers you really do need the help of an older Christian, so pluck up all your courage and . . . GO FOR IT!

Think about it

1 What will be your response if you get invited to play 'Ouija', have your palm read or use tarot cards?

2 Do you know anyone who is involved in these sorts of things? Pray that God would protect them from the evil spiritual powers that they are contacting.

Remember — you are not alone

Twice a week we have an assembly and, as a rule, assemblies are about the only occasions that Christianity gets a mention at school. (I suppose RE lessons would be the only exception to this rule, but when you've got an RE teacher that doesn't believe in the existence of God and thinks that Jesus was an astronaut there's a limit to how 'Christian' Religious Education really can be!)

Anyway, Friday's assembly is a 'whole school' event held in the school sports hall. As soon as the bell goes for the start of school we go to our tutor group rooms to drop off our bags and coats and then make straight for the hall. Arriving at the sports hall door we all (all being the 984 pupils in the school) remove our shoes and walk to the half square metre of floor allocated for each pupil, taking our shoes with us.

It took the combined brain power of the

teachers quite a few weeks to arrive at this simple routine for getting into Friday assembly. The very first week we ever tried it (just after the sports hall had been built), the instruction was to go straight to the sports hall when the bell rang for the start of school. Understandably, perhaps, the novelty of a new event in the school's weekly calendar caused quite a stir, and about half of the school (the younger, more excitable half) arrived at the sports hall early, before the supervising teachers had arrived from their early morning staff briefing. They charged straight into the hall, leaving muddy trails from their shoes all across the new sports hall floor and, using their bags as improvised seating, proceeded to sit down still wrapped in their coats.

At this point Mr Wilson the Strict Deputy Head arrived (every school with more than one Deputy Head has a 'Strict' one for telling you off and keeping order in assemblies, and a 'Friendly' one for helping you when you've been bullied). He surveyed the scene of human chaos and the mud patch that used to be the floor, raised his voice above the high-pitched din and yelled 'Who told you to come in here, you silly children? Get out immediately and take your bags with you.' He was, I think, not happy.

In fact, such was the sheer awesomeness of Mr Wilson's fury that, as one person, the whole assembled mass headed for the door at top speed. Unfortunately, just as they began to beat their hasty retreat, the bell for the start of school rang. This signalled the arrival of the half of the school that had NOT been early for assembly, who tried to enter the sports hall at the same time as the half that had just been thrown out tried to exit. Since the new arrivals were, in the main, larger than those trying to leave, the contest was not an even one and quite soon there was the distinct possibility of serious injury being inflicted on the departing seventh and eighth year pupils.

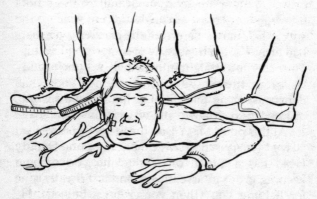

There was the distinct possibility of serious injury being inflicted on the departing pupils.

Mr Wilson soon had the situation under control, however, and managed to get the whole school lining up in one of the four corridor approaches to the sports hall. New instructions were issued. Coats, bags and shoes were to be left in the corridors and not brought in to the hall.

There was a sense of urgency about proceedings now (the fifteen minute assembly time was more than half over already) so everyone duly dropped bags, coats and shoes where they were, filed into the sports hall and sat on the floor for the assembly.

Mr Wilson, who was still almost beside himself with rage, spoke first. He spoke with the sort of quietly threatening tone that you ignored at your peril. He told us terrible tales of people being crushed in crowds, of school finances being wasted on unnecessary floor cleaning bills and of 'softies' who needed seats when there was a perfectly good floor to sit on (all the teachers were sat on chairs around the edge of the sports hall at this point, but I don't think they took it personally). We all felt suitably got at.

The Head, who had obviously prepared a lengthy moralising talk for this historic first assembly in the new sports hall rose to his feet just as the bell for the end of assembly rang. He glanced nervously at his watch and made a hasty decision. 'Because of your ridiculous behaviour this morning I shall save most of what I wanted to say until next week, when I hope that we can have a more ordered start to the school assembly. However I would like to leave you with something to think about during the day. It's from the Bible, actually, and it would have formed a small part of what I wanted to say to you this morning; "Don't make friends with people who have hot, violent tempers. You might learn their habits and not be able to change." ' Everyone's eyes shifted to Mr Wilson and wondered . . . !

We were hastily dismissed and only then did the staff realise the problems caused by 984 pupils searching for shoes, bags and coats in school corridors that looked like the after-effects of an explosion in an Oxfam shop. It was 9.45 before the last person was reunited with their property and it was rumoured that Mr Wilson took the rest of the day off to recover!

So there it was; our week's religious input. To be honest it didn't do much to encourage me to live for Jesus and I don't think it did anything at all for my non-Christian friends.

Bible bit

Is that the way that God intends it? The entire school's Christian input restricted to two Bible verses on a Friday morning and the opinions of an RE teacher who doesn't even believe in God? No, it's not!

A Bible passage that I sometimes imagine might have been set in a school playground (or assembly hall) is found in Matthew 9:36–38. Jesus has been travelling around and has got quite a reputation from his preaching and healing exploits. So many people wanted to get close to him that wherever he went he was followed by a crowd of people.

Perhaps you or I might have got fed up with all the attention and been tempted to tell the crowds to go home and leave us alone. But not so Jesus.

'As Jesus saw the crowds, his heart was filled with pity for them because they were worried and helpless, like sheep without a shepherd.' He was really concerned for the crowds because he knew that he was their only hope. If he turned and walked away from them, they had no one else to go to for help, advice and healing. I think that if Jesus stood in your school and looked around at the crowds he would feel exactly the same.

He would see loads of young people who are trying

to learn how to make sense of life, trying to sort out what is right and what is wrong, trying to understand who they are and how to get on with people around them. The trouble is they are trying to understand life – life that was invented by God – without knowing much or anything at all about the inventor. It's a bit like trying to put together a Lego Technic kit without the instruction leaflet or cook a complicated meal without a recipe book; let's face it, it can't be done! In just the same way, a school full of people who have no real idea about life's inventor and designer are not likely to make a very wonderful job of sorting out what life IS all about – and they are certainly NOT going to be helped by two unexplained Bible verses in a weekly assembly!

So what can be done? Well, in the passage from Matthew's book about the life and times of Jesus, he tells us that after Jesus had been moved to pity for the lost-ness of the crowd, he turned to his best friends and said:

> 'The harvest is large, but there are few workers to gather it in. Pray to the owner of the harvest [God] that he will send out workers to gather in his harvest.'

God's plan is for ordinary Christian people (the workers) to help the harvest (people who don't know God) to know who God is. Putting it more simply, it's all down to you and me! God's plan for introducing himself to people in your school involves YOU and all the other Christians in your school in starring roles.

God wants you to be so full of Jesus that you actually start acting like him. The things that you do become the things that he would do. The things that you say would be the things that he would say. The people that you hang around with would be the people that he would hang around with . . . and so on. If all the Christians in your school started acting like Jesus, then people wouldn't be dependent upon an occasional Christian assembly to teach them about God. In every class in every school there would be walking, talking visual aids showing what God thinks, does and says.

I must be absolutely honest though and say that it's not always going to be easy to try to live for Jesus at school. You see, in a school where most people are not living for Jesus it will soon become obvious that you are different and not everybody will agree with what you believe. Some will say so: others may just ignore you. What does make living for Jesus at school a lot easier is to know that you are not alone; that there are other Christians who agree with what you believe and who can maybe encourage you when the going gets a bit tough. It makes a lot of sense to meet with these other Christians so that you can all know and encourage one another. Perhaps the best way to ensure that this happens regularly is to form a Christian group of some sort which meets in your school, maybe at lunch-time.

If your school already has a Christian group, get involved with it. If it hasn't you may like to consider starting one. Here's some help to get you going. . . .

Practical pointers and handy hints

1   Write to Scripture Union in Schools, 130 City Road, London EC1V 2NJ. Explain who you are and what you want to do. They will be able to send you some

materials to give you a plan for getting started and to help you think through the two important questions:

1. 'What is a school Christian group for?'

and

2. 'What sort of group do we need at our school?'

2 Make a list of as many Christians as you know at your school. Include pupils, teachers – even caretakers and dinner ladies if you know they are Christians.

3 Try to talk to some of the people on your list to explain that you're thinking of starting a Christian group in school. Explain what's in your mind and ask whether they'd be interested in helping start it or being a part of it when it gets going.

4 Talk to your church leader or youth leader and ask them for advice and prayer support.

5 Now the biggie! You will need to see the Head to ask him or her for permission to meet in school and for a room to meet in. If you have a sympathetic teacher then their help will be really useful at this stage.

6 If you get the green light from the Head, then get together with any friends who are ready to help and any teachers who have offered support to discuss what should happen at your first meeting. This is really, really mega-important, because if you get off to a disorganised start then you'll find it hard to recover. The Scripture Union materials should be especially helpful at this stage (point 1 above).

7 Having organised it, you need to publicise it. Perhaps write personal invitations to all the Christians that you know in the school. (If you can provide free biscuits or food at the first meeting it may encourage a few more to come!)

8 When you've organised and publicised, all you can do is wait and pray! When the first meeting happens someone needs to explain to the people there (and don't be discouraged if there are fewer that you'd hoped for) what the Christian group is all about and why it's important to have a group in school. The two main reasons are

   1.   TO ENCOURAGE THE CHRISTIANS,

and to

   2.   INTRODUCE ANY NON-CHRISTIANS TO JESUS.

9 Try to be as enthusiastic as possible (enthusiasm is catching!) and take the names of everyone who came and ask them if they know of any other Christians to invite to the next meeting.

10 Soon after the first meeting, get together with your planning group again and talk about what should happen next. (Again, the Scripture Union materials will be very useful.)

Think about it

1 If Jesus came to your school:

(a) who would he feel pity for?
(b) who would he spend time with?
(c) who or what would upset him?
(d) who or what would please him?

(e) what would he say to your friends?

2 How like Jesus in school are YOU in school?

Outro

Here are ten assorted uses for this book:

1 Rip it into tiny pieces and throw it at the bride and groom at the next wedding you see.

2 Put it into a food processor, add water and make *Chocolate Teapot* soup.

3 Sit on it all night.

4 Put it inside your trainers and run around the garden.

5 Tie it to a short stick and use it as a badminton racquet.

6 Take it back to the shop that you bought it from and ask for your money back.

7 Put it into a video player and watch it.

8 Give it to someone that you don't like very much.

9 Plant it in a Gro-bag and water it every day.

10 Introduce it to your pet gerbil.

Alternatively you could read it and then spend some time thinking about it! If you have read the book, go back and have a quick look at the 'Bible bit' and the 'Think about it' section in each chapter. You'll probably find that there are some bits that you've almost forgotten about already, but other bits are still quite fresh in your mind. In case you're wondering why that is, I'm going to tell you!

When you read a book like this God wants to speak to you through what it says. Don't forget that God knows you inside out, so he knows what you need. As you've been reading this book God has been telling the Holy Spirit to make the bits that are especially important for you to stick in your mind. So the parts that you can remember are possibly parts that God really wants you to hear **AND do something about!**

The real value of this book to you is if it helps you live more confidently as a Christian in school. God wants to help you do that, but you must play your part. This book has given you quite a bit of practical advice – things to actually DO. But you can't do everything all at once, so start with just one thing – maybe your attitude to teachers, or your willingness to speak up for Jesus: whatever is a problem for you at the moment – and get stuck into sorting that one thing out.

After a period of time you'll feel that things have improved a bit in that area (we hope!), so flick through the book again and start trying to work at another area.

If you're normal you won't have enjoyed this book much(!) – but apart from that you will also continue to get things wrong occasionally. Don't give up at the first mistake; ask God to forgive you and help you to start all over again. **Don't be a Chocolate Teapot, melting away when the heat's turned up at school; stand up for God and know that he loves you enough to help you through each day, however hot it gets.**